willow

cocoa

orange

coconut

date

mangrove

beech

papaya

sycamore

oyamel

joshua

oak

holly

pear

For everyone who loves trees

Mandy

First published in 2023 by Child's Play (International) Ltd
Ashworth Road, Bridgemead, Swindon SN5 7YD, UK

Published in USA in 2023 by Child's Play Inc
250 Minot Avenue, Auburn, Maine 04210

Distributed in Australia by Child's Play Australia Pty Ltd
Unit 10/20 Narabang Way, Belrose, Sydney, NSW 2085

ISBN 978-1-78628-682-6
SJ010922CPL12226826

Printed and bound in Shenzhen, China

1 3 5 7 9 10 8 6 4 2

A catalogue record of this book is available from the British Library

www.childs-play.com

Tree Whispers

Mandy Ross

illustrated by Juliana Oakley

Whispering Trees

We trees are giants,
joining earth and sky.
Hundreds of years
growing deep and high.
Our leaves rustle,
our roots whisper.
Shhh... listen...
If you were a tree,
what would you whisper to me?

Can You Be a Tree?

Legs for your trunk,
rooted right there,
arms for branches,
waving in the air,
and all the flying birds,
making nests in your hair.

So Many Different, Beautiful Ways to Be

Tall
or small
or in between,
leafy or bare
or evergreen,
soft or spiky,
swaying or still,
on a city street
or alone on a hill,
or side by side
in a forest family.
So many different,
beautiful ways
to be
a tree.
Or you.
Or me.

Tree's Storm Song

Ssswoooooshhh swish-swoo-ooo-ooosh,
cree-eee-eak, creak, squeak, groan,
drip-drip-drip, drop, drip,
rustle-rustle-rustle-rustle-rustle,
Shhh-sh-shhhhhh!
Whoooh whoosh-whish-whoooooosh whooo-hoooh!
Shhh...

Translation:
Oh, wind and rain music! Stormy greetings to my leafy companions!
We dance together. See how the young ones bend flexibly.
Drink the rain. You will grow strong.
Welcome little birds. Rest safe, close to my trunk.
No humans walking below today. I wonder why?
Ah, here they come now, their waterproof coverings flapping.
Shhh...

Trees Breathe

Breathe in...
Breathe out...
We breathe in...
We breathe out...
Every tree, wood, forest, jungle,
we're the giant, green lungs of the earth,
your vast planetary breathing system.
We turn air into heartwood,
transform light to leaf,
rain to roots to leaf to cloud.
We capture carbon,
breathe out oxygen.
Don't stop us!
Don't chop us!
Stand with us!
Breathe with us!

Breathe in...
Breathe out...

Breathe in...   Breathe out...

Breathe in...   Breathe out...

Breathe in...   Breathe out...

Shinrin-Yoku:
How to Go Forest Bathing

Where?
Right here!
In this forest, this wood,
or beneath this very tree.

When?
Right now!
Whatever the weather,
dawn or dusk, noon or night.

What shall I bring?
Bring your eyes, ears, nose,
hands, feet, lungs, heart.
Whatever you can bring!
Bring yourself! Ready?

Let's go forest bathing...
in sunshine or moonlight dappling,
in sound of rain, drip-drop-dripping,
in wind rustling and creatures moving,
in sky-vastness above
and earth-stillness beneath your feet.

The Naming of Trees

Do you know the name of this tree?
No? Nor does the tree.
Let's make one up!

Measure-How-You've-Grown Tree

Knock-Knock-Peck-Peck Tree

Welcome Shade Tree

Growing-Between-The-Toes Tree

Looks-Like-An-Elephant Tree

How Trees Talk

Overground forest, a brave, green family,
old giants sheltering bright, young saplings,
sharing goodness and rain to grow tall
and strong in a leafy, lively, wood-wise hug.

While shhh... in the underforest otherworld,
creeping deep among roots and rootlets,
threads and microscopic shootlets
spinning and weaving a wood-wide web
of silent messages, urgently whispering,
"Share! Grow! Breathe! Listen!
We protect you! Protect us!"

Secret City

Under the earth, among the roots,
it's deep, deep, dark, both day and night.
Beneath the trees we burrow
and tunnel a secret city, out of sight.

In the dark, down here, we're safe and snug.
We tell bedtime stories of moon and sun
up above, where the sky is deep,
and when we're tired of tunnels –
then we sleep.

City Trees

Deep in the forest, long ago,
the first humans lived among the trees.

Deep in the city, now,
trees live among the humans.

Branches reaching over fences and roofs,
waving above our streets and schools,
bewitching light into leaf and wood,
breathing the sky and the air we share.

Weeds or Seeds?

Don't call us weeds!
We're the niftiest seeds!
In a wasteland place by the railway tracks
or tiny gaps and pavement cracks,
we tuck and squeeze
to grow our roots
and small green shoots,
fresh and free,
aiming to be
great, big, strong trees
to grow more seeds!

Sycamore and Seeds

Sycamore says,
"I'm tall and strong, my branches wide,
sprouting thousands of seeds, my babies!
Ready to whirl on the swirling winds.
Goodbye, goodbye! Away you fly!"

Sycamore's seeds say,
"Goodbye, goodbye! Away we fly
to whirl and twirl on the swirling winds
to find a place to grow, until
we're tall and strong, our branches wide..."

Willow

Waving willow, growing quickly,
tall and spreading, green and thirsty!
Plant it where the water's plenty,
keep from flooding when it's stormy,
hold the riverbank, strong and sturdy.

Willow basket, fishnet weaving,
willow medicine, aching, soothing.
Need a fence? Plant one living!
Lovely leafy sculpture growing.
What a wonder, willow waving!

"Who's That?" asks the Oak

"Who's that, tickling my branches?" asks the oak.

The busy blackbird says, "It's me,
building a nest for my babies."

"Who's that, tickling my trunk?" asks the oak.

The scampering squirrel says, "It's me,
hungry for acorns for dinner."

"Who's that, tickling my bark?" asks the oak.

The woodpecker pecks, "It's me,
peckish for bugs for dinner."

"And who's that, tickling between my toes?" asks the oak.

And all the bugs and beetles, creepers and crawlers whisper,
"It's us, safe between your toes.
We don't want to be anyone's dinner!"

Where Do You Sleep?

Do you rest your head
on a little round bed
of twigs and moss
and mud and grass
at the top of a tree,
with stars to see,
high and deep
to rock you to sleep?
East, west, a nest is best.

Tiny Things to Find

Kneeling down,
muddy knees,
right up close...
Can you find all these?

A blade of grass,
a rootlet reaching up,
a tree's seed,
an acorn's egg cup,
a ladybird's spots,
a line of ants,
a micro-tree in a leaf?

What other tiny things
can you find?

Sounds and Movement

Still or moving?
Loud or silent?
Who's making that sound?
You, me, creature, earth or tree?

Wind in the trees,
boots crunching through crackly leaves,
birds' wings flapping,
stream trickling,
river rushing,
rain drip-dropping,
twig snapping,
puddle splashing.

What else is moving around you?

Making Art Together

Twigs and sticks,
leaves and seeds.
Tree gives, you gather,
making art together.

A straight line, a wiggly line,
a circle or a square,
a letter, a word,
a pattern or a picture,
a mark, an arrow,
a patch of green,
a secret sign,
a gift to spy
for someone passing by.

What else can you make?

Made by Magic

Special moments,
tracks and traces,
secret codes, wild surprises.

What else might be made by magic?

A tree's eye in a trunk,
blue sky in a puddle,
raindrops hanging on a spider's web,
bird footprints in the mud,
a carpet of pink blossom,
a flock of birds flying together,
red sky, a rainbow.

What other magical things can you notice?

Dream the World's an Orchard

Can you dream
the world's an orchard,
buzzing with bees
in the fruit salad trees,
growing the sweetest treats...?
Apple trees,
banana, orange,
pear, pomegranate,
peach, papaya,
lemon, mango,
dates, coconuts...
and cocoa!

Snow Forest

Once upon a winter,
when the snow lies deep,
deer peep and wolves creep.
Glimpse a cardinal, a red cape,
a firebird's feather,
and a little snow mouse
by the forester's house.
Footprints in the snow.
Time to go!

Hanami Picnic

Winter waiting...
bud burst!
Cheery cherry
soft snow petal
spring magic moment.
Plan perfect pink picnic
beneath blossom.
Hanami happiness!

Baobab

I'm the shady baobab, famous far around,
with a huge, strong trunk, fat and round.
Stories say I'm planted upside down,
roots in the sky and head in the ground.

But I'm the right way round!
Could it be YOU
who's upside down?

Pando

We are The Trembling Giant, Pando,
bigger than any other trees,
we're ALL these aspen brother-trees.
We're just one being, connected deep down
by a giant spreading root-web under the ground.

We're vastly alive! Eighty thousand years old!
We're a mellow, yellow, joined-up forest,
millions of leaves shimmering, shaking,
a mighty murmuring, bravely quaking.
We are The Trembling Giant, Pando.

Oh, Blue Jacaranda

Oh, blue jacaranda!
Blue treetop fingertips
tickling the blue sky-under.
Oh, blue jacaranda!
What a wonder!
Blue sky, blue cloud,
and a blue carpet under.
Oh, blue jacaranda!

Pine, Oak, Oyamel

Pine, oak, and oyamel trees,
Mexican forest, blue and green.
Millions of monarch butterflies fluttering
thousands of miles from north to south,
till the blue-green forest is dressed
in orange cloaks of butterflies resting.

Joshua Tree

In a thirsty land
of rock and sand,
hot and dry
under a fierce blue sky,
we desert trees grow tall,
spiny, spiky, prickly,
tickled by giant scorpions,
centipedes, millipedes,
lines of ants
and tarantulas scuttling.

Cold are the nights,
but the stars are bright!

Rainforest

Wherever it's hot and wild and wet and dripping,
rainforest trees are alive with creatures,
calling and squawking,
chattering, howling,
hunting, escaping,
eating and gathering,
swinging, gliding,
flying and slithering,
spinning and nesting
and hanging and creeping…
and sleeping.

Can YOU swing from branch to branch,
hang upside down,
glide and slither,
build a nest or a den,
and then…
sleep under a tree?

Land or Sea or In Between?

Mangrove trees in salty water,
roots in muddy tides and currents,
sucking water up trunks and branches,
breathing out into salty air.
Who's here, on land or sea or in between?
Tree snakes, tree frogs, tree kangaroos,
dozing koalas, leaping mudskippers,
gliding stingrays, diving platypuses,
and oh… beware…
crocodiles lurking in between.

Count My Rings

"Though you can't see," breathes the tree,
"invisibly, each day, I'm growing taller and stronger under the sky."

"Though you can't see," breathes the tree,
"invisibly, each year, I'm growing a new ring under my bark."

"Now you can see," whispers the tree.
"Count my rings, count my years. They're visible – after you chop!"

"Then my growing… stops."

Tree Spell

Patter, rain.
Shine, sun.
Rustle, wind.
Steady, earth.
Keep safe the creatures in our branches.

Loathe fire.
Dread drought.
Curse axe.
Jinx digger.
Danger for the creatures in our branches.

If you chop,
if you clear,
forest gone,
then you'll fear!
Just like the creatures in our branches.

Plant a Tree

Plant a seed,
plant a tree,
plant a forest,
plant the future.

See this tree?
A hundred years ago,
two hundred,
or maybe three,
someone did...
plant a seed,
plant a tree,
plant a forest,
plant the future,
for people not yet born,
for you and for me.

So let's...
plant a seed,
plant a tree,
plant a forest,
plant the future,
for people not yet born,
AND for you and for me!

pando

blue jacaranda

date

mangrove

willow

orange

pear

banana

pine

papaya

maple

hazel

cocoa